IS THERE ANYBODY OUT THE WALL?

By Luis Carlos Molina Acevedo

Title: Is There Anybody Out The Wall?

First edition

Copyright © 2016 Luis Carlos Molina Acevedo

© Texts: Luis Carlos Molina Acevedo

Author: Luis Carlos Molina Acevedo

Contact: lcmolinaa@yahoo.es

http://lcmolinaa.blogspot.com

Cover design: Luis Carlos Molina Acevedo

Style Review: Luis Carlos Molina Acevedo

ISBN-13: 978-1523629749

ISBN-10: 1523629746

About the Author

Luis Carlos Molina Acevedo was born in Fredonia, Colombia. He is Social Communicator of the University of Antioquia, and Masters in Linguistics from the same university. The author has published more than twenty books online bookstores:

I Want to Fly, From Don Juan to Sexual Vampirism, The Imaginary of Exaggeration, The Clavicle of Dreams, For Writers by Writers, The Modern Concept of Communication, and Is There Anybody Out The Wall?.

Quiero Volar, El Alfarero de Cuentos, Virtuales Sensaciones, El Abogado del Presidente, Guayacán Rojo Sangre, Territorios de Muerte, Años de Langosta, El Confesor, El Orbe Llamador, Oscares al Desnudo, Diez Cortos Animados, La Fortaleza, Tribunal Inapelable, Operación Ameba, Territorios de la Muerte, La Edad de la Langosta, Del Donjuanismo al Vampirismo Sexual, Imaginaria de la Exageración, La Clavícula de los Sueños, Quince Escritores Colombianos, De Escritores para Escritores, El Moderno Concepto de Comunicación, Sociosemántica de la Amistad, Magia: Símbolos y Textos de la Magia, ¿Hay Alguien Afuera del Muro?.

Content

IN THE WALL...1

   Movie Synopsis: 3

   Technical Sheet of Movie........................3

   Does anyone here remember Vera Lynn? 5

   The name Pink Floyd...............................7

   About Pink Floyd 9

   Studio albums...12

   About the album The Wall.....................15

   About the Film "Pink Floyd The Wall"............17

IS THERE ANYBODY OUT THE WALL? 21

   The double doors 23

   The wall of the classroom 27

   The door of the caravan 29

   Destroyed apartment window 31

   The destroyed TV screen 33

   The free fall in the pool.........................35

   The lively shell of doom.........................37

The wall explodes into pieces 39

Television 41

The telephone 45

THE REAL 49

The hotel corridor 53

The hotel room 55

Emergency stairs 63

The limousine 65

THE MEMORY 67

With the mother 69

At school 71

With friends 75

In the House 77

In the park 79

In the ballroom 81

THE IMAGINATION 83

The father in the war 85

Imagined childhood 87

The unfaithful wife 89

Animated concepts 91

THE DESIRE 97

Marriage 99

The world 101

Pleasure 103

Mental oasis 105

The dictator 109

IS THERE ANYBODY IN THE WALL? 115

Wife 117

The dirty woman 119

Manager 121

Bibliography 123

Presentation

IS THERE ANYBODY OUT THE WALL? is an analysis of the movie "Pink Floyd The Wall". For this study, it is considered the film as revolving around two basic questions: "Is there anybody out there?" and "Is there anybody in there?" With the first starts this process of interpretation. And with the second ends this assay.

It is considered, in addition, that the film is a mental machine to travel back in time. It consists of four levers: the real, memories, imagination, and desire. The first allows travelling in present time. The second allows travelling in past time. The third allows travelling in possible time, potential. And the fourth allows travelling in future time.

Thanks Pink Floyd by make my life more bearable. In moments of disappointment toward the world, toward life, always I have returned to his songs. His high notes immediately have connected my nervous system with the cosmos, with the universe. Thanks for the spatial connection. For me, the screams of the vocal cords, to extend the duration of guitar notes beyond the usual, are the portal to cross the wall.

IN THE WALL

In the movie "Pink Floyd The Wall" there are two basic questions:

1. Is There Anybody Out There?

2. Is There Anybody In There?

These two questions structured the content. Both songs and the images of the film are arranged to respond to those two questions.

The wall in the film symbolizes the mind. The mind, in turn, in the film, is a mental time machine. This time machine is operated with four levers, according to where musician want to go:

1. The Real

2. The memories

3. The Imagination

4. The Desire

The real lever allows travel through time present. It consists of everything that happens around the singer Pink, in his hotel before the concert.

The lever of the memories allows travel into the past time. It consists of the experiences of Pinky, the singer, when he was a child.

The lever of the imagination allows travel through potential time. It consists of all none witnessed by Pink, but re-created by him as part of his mental world.

The lever of the desire allows travel through future time. It consists of the aspirations of Pink, that is, it is everything which should happen in time to come.

About how they are expressed these two questions in the film and the four levers for mental time travel, it tries this text. But before going on, let's see some basic information about the film and the group.

Movie Synopsis:

Pink, the singer of a band lives from childhood a series of traumas due to the harsh upbringing. He tired of all that surrounds his profession and takes refuge in drugs as the only option to break the wall, created by him. (With summaries like these, it is promoted commercially the film).

Technical Sheet of Movie

Metro - Goldwing Mayer Presents

An Alan Parker Film

Pink Floyd The Wall by Roger Waters

Designed by Gerald Scarfe

Key Animator Mike Stuart

Produced by Alan Marshall

Original Music From the album "The Wall" Produced by Bob Ezrin, David Gilmour, James Guthrie, Roger Waters

"The Little Boy That Santa Claus Forgot" sung by Vera Lynn

© 1982 by MGM / UA Entertainment Co.

Made at Pinewood Studios, London, England, by Tin Blue Ltd in association with Films Goldcrest

Duration: 95:06

At this point, I should point out something important. The affirmations made from here until the end of this chapter "On the Wall", they are based on the bibliography included at the end of this book.

Does anyone here remember Vera Lynn?

That is the question posed in the film when the surviving soldiers are returning from war. Pinky is at the train station. He looks for his father among those present. This question sounds strange in the context of what it had seen the spectator before and what he will see after. It seems a question unrelated. In the film, there are not the necessary references for the spectator. It is a void in the story. Perhaps the British persons of 55 years old, at the time of release of the film, know for sure why the question is done. For the other people, it is difficult. Maybe one person restless of audience, after to leave the theatre, inquiries who was Vera Lynn, then, he will know:

Vera Lynn was born with the name of Vera Margaret Welch on March 20, 1917 in East Ham, London. She later adopted the surname of her grandmother, Lynn. She began singing at the age of 7 years in a club for workers. In 1940 she started her own radio show, "Sincerely Yours". She sent messages to British troops stationed abroad. In this show she and a quartet interpreted the songs most requested by soldiers abroad.

In the film it is made a reference to the song "We'll Meet Again". With this song, the singer does a kind of promise to soldiers in the war. Somehow, they return to meet her. The question at the train station is quite a claim by Pinky due the unfulfilled promise. His father is not there.

Does anybody here remember Vera Lynn?

Remember how she said that

We would meet again

Some sunny day?

Vera! Vera!

What has become of you?

Does anybody else in here

Feel the way I do?

The film begins with the song "The Little Boy That Santa Claus Forgot". Here the singer talks about another broken promise, this time by Santa Claus. He forgot to bring gifts to Pinky (little Pink), despite he not asks for much and he had behaved well.

The name Pink Floyd

As usual, Pink Floyd was born from several musical efforts of their members in various groupings. It all started in 1964 with a group called "Sigma 6". Then, the group "Tea Set" was formed. In this, it met for the first time Roger Waters, Nick Mason, Richard Wright, and Syd Barrett. This name was kept for long. Then, in a concert of bands, they came together with another group of the same name and they decided take the name of "The Pink Floyd Sound".

"The Pink Floyd Sound" came from combining the names of two bluesmen, Pink Anderson and Floyd Council. After, for ease, the group began to call themselves "The Pink Floyd". With the arrival of guitarist David Gilmour, he always spoke of "Pink Floyd" and the group ended up with this name. With this name, the group was known in the world.

Luis Carlos Molina Acevedo

About Pink Floyd

Initially, the group was formed by drummer Nick Mason, keyboardist and vocalist Richard Wright, bassist and vocalist Roger Waters and guitarist and main vocalist Syd Barrett, who became the first leader of the band. Bob Klose was initially guitarist for a short time, but did not appear in any album. Barrett, led by the stress of the art world, began to use drugs, especially LSD. At concerts, he began to have gaps. In December 1967, it was invited his friend David Gilmour to support him as a vocalist and guitarist. The situation of Barrett worsened. He left the group in April 1968 and thus, the classic formation of the group was defined.

The career of the group has been classified into three stages. Each stage marked by the leader of the group at that moment. The first phase marked by Syd Barrett. The second was led by Roger Waters. And the third was undertaken by David Gilmour. Each stage marked a particular style.

Led by Waters, the group recorded many albums. They became great commercial successes such as The Dark Side of the Moon (1973) Wish You Were Here

(1975) Animals (1977) and The Wall (1979). During the recording sessions of The Wall, bassist Roger Waters dismissed to Rick Wright of the band. The keyboardist was not making appropriate contributions to the album, in consideration of Waters. In 1983, the group released the album The Final Cut. It had a modest success compared to his earlier works and even, the band did not tour. In 1985, Waters declared Pink Floyd extinction. In his opinion, the band was exhausted creatively.

The other members, Gilmour and Mason, refused to accept the decision of Waters and continued with the group. Waters sued, claiming the rights of brand Pink Floyd. He lost in court. He reached an agreement with Gilmour and Mason. He obtained exclusive rights to all the imagery displayed on the concerts, including the famous flying pig, and the rights to the audiovisual show of The Wall, excluding three songs that Gilmour had compound: "Young Lust", "Run Like Hell" and "Comfortably Numb". He also obtained the rights to all songs on The Final Cut. Of this way, the rest of the group could continue to use the name Pink Floyd smoothly.

Waters, meanwhile, embarked on a solo career and he was not reunited with Pink Floyd until 24 years later, on July 2, 2005, at the Live 8 concert in London, where they played songs Speak to Me, Breathe, Money, Wish You Were Here and Comfortably Numb.

In November 2014, it was released The Endless River, the last studio album of the band. It contains material largely recorded during the recording sessions of The Division Bell from 1993 to 1994 without any contribution from Roger Waters.

The group was always concerned about having the best sound technology available. At first, they were notable for the use of stereo panning, tape editing, echo effects tape and using electronic keyboards, including a Farfisa organ played by Wright. They incorporated, into their works, noise, sound effects, percussion, tape loops and oscillators. For example, "Several Species of Small Furry Animals Gathered Together in a Cave and Grooving with a Pict" is a five-minute song. It presents only to Waters singing with his voice at different speeds, resulting in something like the sound of birds and rodents. Another song, "Alan's Psychedelic Breakfast", is a sound collage of a man who cooks and eats his breakfast, meanwhile in the background, his thoughts sound accompanied by instrumental lines.

The different styles of each of the composers converged into a single. It crystallized in the two most important works of his discography, to critics and audiences: The Dark Side of the Moon (1973) and Wish You Were Here (1975). In both works, Gilmour became the lead singer of the group. The female choirs and Dick Parry's saxophone acquired special relevance.

The Dark Side of the Moon became the first number one of the band and one of the best sellers in the history of the United States to exceed fifteen million copies sold. It was also one of the most sold worldwide, with more than forty million copies. It remained in the Billboard 200 for 741 weeks, a record at that time, including 591 in a row from 1976 to

1988. This meant another record. One in four British households has a copy of the album in any of its formats, according to the estimate. It also stayed in the UK charts for 301 weeks, but never surpassed the second place. Its cover contains a prism to represent the phenomenon of light scattering. It was designed by Storm Thorgerson and Audrey Powell. Almost all covers of Pink Floyd were designed by Thorgerson.

"Wish You Were Here" (1975) was the first album to reach the top spot in the UK and in the US, and it was equally praised by critics as before it was "The Dark Side of the Moon". "Money", contained in the latter album, is considered the single record most famous of rock in the world and the best-selling, along with the album.

The band adopted Steve O'Rourke as manager, who would go on with Pink Floyd until his death in 2003.

Perhaps the female singer, in choir, most important of band was Durga McBroom.

Studio albums

05/08/1967: The Piper at the Gates of Dawn

29/06/1968: A Saucerful of Secrets

07/27/1969: Music from the Film More

25/10/1969: Ummagumma

10/10/1970: Atom Heart Mother

30/10/1971: Meddle

03/06/1972: Obscured by Clouds

03/24/1973: The Dark Side of the Moon

09/15/1975: Wish You Were Here

Is There Anybody Out The Wall?

23/01/1977: Animals
30/11/1979: The Wall
23/03/1983: The Final Cut
07/09/1987: A Momentary Lapse of Reason
30/03/1994: The Division Bell
10/11/2014: The Endless River

About the album The Wall

The epic opera of rock The Wall was released in 1979. It was composed almost entirely by Waters. It addresses issues of loneliness and lack of communication. The idea stems from the metaphor of separation between musicians and their audience. This metaphor was symbolized by a wall. It is built between the musician and the audience. Waters devised this format when he spat at a fanatical person in a concert in Montreal, Canada. With "The Wall", Pink Floyd returned to the top of the charts with the single "Another Brick in the Wall, Part II". The 340 thousand copies distributed in the UK were sold in just five days. "Comfortably Numb" and "Run Like Hell" also became classics of the group and the radio stations without having been published as singles. "The Wall" was praised by critics and won 23 platinum albums, selling 11.5 million copies in the US.

.

About the Film "Pink Floyd The Wall"

The film "Pink Floyd The Wall" was made in 1982. The soundtrack is made up of most of the content of the album "The Wall". The film was written by Waters and was directed by Alan Parker. The main actor was Bob Geldof, founder of the group Boomtown Rats. He re-recorded many of the vocal parts of the original album. The theme of the film is based on some experiences of Syd Barrett (Pink Adult) and Roger Waters (Pink child). The animation of it was conducted by Gerald Scarfe. The song "When the Tigers Broke Free" first appeared in this film. After, it was published as a single of limited edition. But it became popular when it was included in the compilation "Echoes: The Best of Pink Floyd" and the second edition of The Final Cut. Another original song of the film is "What Shall We Do Now?" It was removed from the original album due to the time constraints of vinyl records. The only songs from "The Wall" and not used in the film were "Hey You" and "The Show Must Go On".

One of the recurring themes of film is the death of the father of Pink. The theme is inspired by the death of Waters' father, Eric Fletcher Waters, killed in action in World War II. Waters at that time was still in the womb. His mother was five months pregnant.

The filming for the movie began with Gerald Scarfe and Michael Seresin as co-directors, and Alan Parker as overall producer. After a week, the work did not advance. Alan Parker was promoted to director. Michael departed, but Gerald was assigned to other duties.

Bob Geldof was at first reluctant to accept the lead role of Pink in the film. He does not like the Pink Floyd, as he called them. After accepting, he was upset because the script had no dialogues for him. Once heavily involved in the work, he gave the best of him. Alan Parker was surprised when he agreed to shave his head and eyebrows. The actor could not swim. For that, the scenes in the pool are very authentic, in the Director's view. The actor was dissatisfied only when he had to undress in a cold night to make a scene at a biscuit factory in Hammersmith. His body should be covered in pink slime and asked to metamorphose into a fascist.

Another anecdote was starred the actress with the role of dirty woman in the apartment of Pink. She asked to the director: what is the motivation to feel me threatened by Pink? And he said: "The money."

The battle sequences were shot at Saunton Sands in Devon. For the scenes, two aircraft half-scale Stuka were used. One worked perfectly. A certified pilot had to control it. The other crashed into the sea. Another scenario was the Royal Horticultural Hall. He met a group of two thousand skinheads with which the concert scenes and political rallies were filmed. The Choreographer Gillian Gregory should teach basic dance steps to the skinheads, but she withdrew shortly after seeing the lack of natural coordination in them. They were to march in unison and it not was possible.

The sign on the door of Alan Parker at Pinewood Studios said: "Just Another Prick On The Wall." He not had disagreements with Roger Waters. Waters was satisfied with the outcome of the film. The producer, Alan Marshall, was asked what the meaning of the film was and he replied: "It's about some mad bastard and this wall, innit…"

In an interview, Roger Waters said, "Goodbye Blue Sky" is a song about Pink, leaving his home to seek his own path.

Pink watches on TV an old war movie called "The Dam Busters". It is the biography of Barnes Wallis. He invented the bouncing bomb. This was launched by bombers into water reserves. Slowly it sank to finally explode, breaking levees and flooding the valleys where the German steel industry was settled. This, it paralyzed the industry and prevented the production of steel needed for war.

What built by Pink in his hotel room is still a mystery. In an interview, Roger Waters declares "Is There Anybody Out There" is a piece only necessary to create an atmosphere of isolation. What built by Pink in the film, according to several analysts, it is a replica of army barricades with bunkers and corridors.

The scene in "Run Like Hell", for some, is a recreation of an event called "Kristallnacht" (the night of broken glass) occurred in Hitler's Germany.

The Nazis smashed windows of Jewish businesses. The term comes from the broken glass in the streets. They glistened under the moonlight.

The sequence of fascist Pink, it is perhaps one that most confusion causes among spectators. It is an unexpected change in the behaviour of the singer. Many interpretations have been tried to explain this part of the film. One of them states: The fascist character may be based on a British politician named Sir Oswald Mosely. He established the British Fascist Party. Its sign was a megaphone. Some of their slogans can be recognized in "Waiting for the Worms".

IS THERE ANYBODY OUT THE WALL?

The film, Pink Floyd The Wall, seems to ask two questions unanswered. One of them: Is there anyone out the wall? This question is for the first time at 54 minutes 15 seconds, after the film started (54:15). Pink jumps. He wants to reach the top of the wall. He is trying to find an exit to the other side of the wall. This happens while playing the song "Is There Anybody Out There?"

As this analysis of the movie "Pink Floyd The Wall" is not linear, I have made some references to time line of the film in the minute-second format (00:00). Thus, the reader will have a precise location about the sequences studied here.

Contrary to what it was seen by the average spectator of the movie, the attempts of Pink to cross to the other side of the wall, are several. It is not only when the wall is collapsed. There are eight attempts to cross toward the other side of the wall:

1. The double door opens to give way to the crowd (5:55).

2. Students demolished a wall of the classroom with the hatchets of the fire cabinet (26:45).

3. Pink goes through the door of his trailer caravan to let come in the dirty woman (43:10).

4. Pink destroys the apartment window and he can cross the wall (48:00).

5. Pink destroys the TV with his guitar (51:30).

6. The free fall in the pool by Pink (12:10, 56:10)

7. During the trial, Pink begins to float in the air. Animated background strikes and it breaks as eggshell. Pink goes into darkness (87:33).

8. The wall explodes into pieces at the end of the film (90:00).

In addition to cross the wall, at least eight times, Pink has contact with the other side of the wall, without the need for cracks, through:

1. The television

2. The telephone

Then, we look at these ten aspects of the question.

The double doors

The woman, of the cleaner at the hotel, looks for the keys to open the room door of Pink. The safety chain inside the door is stirred and merges with the image of another thick chain. This ensures a double wooden door. It stirs the thick chain and a grille falls to make way for a crowd. The thick chain is broken and a crowd crosses the wall through the door collapsed. This sequence, in respect of many analysts, represents the birth of Pink. Here, the interpretation is different.

Independent of the meaning given by the writer of the script, Roger Waters, this scene contains several elements of interpretation. The wall is crossed for the first time. On the other side there is only competition. Some are rolled on the floor while others pass overhead. Outside the wall, there are clashes with police. That is all at the other side of the wall. In short, there is nobody. People are too busy in compete and fight. They can not motivate him to cross the mental wall.

The images of the sequence also allow a different interpretation to the suggested by most analysts. The validity of this other interpretation is given by the poster: "Sports Arena Box Office". The camera shows the post while it takes place the clash with police. This suggests a connection with what was said by Waters and Nick Manson. The two agree about the source element for creating The Wall. The incident when Waters spits at a fanatical person in the concert of Canada, it is the fact of departure for the theme of the album and the movie. At this place, the Olympics had been made the previous year. The poster would refer to this place and what happened there, before, during and after the concert. The doors are open to force by the crowd to enter the stadium early. The sequence refers to what happened before and after the concert. After the concert, it was the confrontation with the police.

This sequence, actually, would not be about the birth of Pink, but about the origin of the film. A mass of fanatics is rampaging without control. Not even the police can control them. So, there must be a wall between fanatics and musicians on stage. This interpretation is all the more valid if one considers the sequence shown before, the father of Pink is preparing to go to war. The two sequences mark the beginning of the film, just with the two thematic elements at the base of this: the abandonment of the father, the recurring theme, and Waters spits a fan, triggering the idea to write the story.

The essence of this sequence as crossing of one side of the wall to the other, it is to recognize how in the other side there is nothing to motivate the passage toward the other side of the wall. Is there anyone out the wall? No one can answer this question. On the other side of the wall there are only beings in open competition and in confrontation with authority. The screams and commotion, created, not allowed anybody to hear the question from the other side of the wall. Pink should look for other means to try reach an answer for his question.

Luis Carlos Molina Acevedo

The wall of the classroom

Students, without face, are removed masks and they roll the desks by the floor. They look for the cabinets for fire prevention. They take the hatchets. They destroy the desks. Then, they hit the walls with them until to tear it down.

Again, there is no one answer to the question from the other side of the wall. Across the wall collapsed there are only more walls, more classrooms. There are more students eating the flesh like worms, to enjoy of the pudding at the end. There are only two roads, or you eat the flesh of the meek persons or you end up being meat for worms. Students end up being ground meat. It is the world of eaters and the ones eaten.

Worms, in the film, is a symbol of the ruling class. It is perhaps another attempt of Waters to symbolize social behaviour of people, more subtle. His first intention was achieved with the album "Animals" and their symbols: pigs, dogs, and sheep. Pigs are the ruling class, dogs are the military class, and sheep are the other people, destined to be fed to pigs and dogs. Waters takes the idea of reading the book "Animal Farm: A Fairy Story" by George Orwell. In several

Luis Carlos Molina Acevedo

sequences of the film the meaning of worms as the ruling class is evident. They suck the meat of others. They exploit to others and so, they receive the pudding at the end.

This sequence raises another failed attempt to cross the wall. Pink is forced to explore other ways to find out if it's worth crossing to the other side of the wall or not. Perhaps the wall does not extend as might be the interpretation to the naked eye. Pink, with each failed attempt, becomes aware of the complexity of the wall. The wall does not extend by construction, but by discovery of its size and complexity. The protagonist knows the true dimensions of the wall, with each attempt to find an answer to his question.

The door of the caravan

The dirty women enter to the parking lot where the trailer for concert tour of Pink is. They seduce to vigilant and access the trailer where the manager and his entourage are. After some images to suggest an orgy, women leave the trailer. Pink is in the window of his trailer. He sees to one of the dirty women. She drinks something. He decides to cross to the other side of the wall. He opens the door. He lowers the three rungs toward the floor. He seeks to be seen by the dirty woman. And of course, she sees him and runs to him. She extends him an album for the autograph. Pink comes back to the trailer. She decides to enter the trailer too.

Of background, it sounds "Young Lust". The woman is shocked to see that place. "This place is bigger than our whole apartment" she says. It was too comfortable to be in a caravan of trailers. She was also surprised with the amount of guitars and the tub in that place.

Again, Pink has a failed attempt to get to the other side of the wall. Perhaps the answer was a dirty woman, a dirty girl. "Oooh! I need a dirty woman.

Oooh! I need a dirty girl", says the lyric of the song. Pink returns to be deceived. The dirty woman is not the answer to his question. She's not on the other side of the wall. She is on this side. She is only the trigger for another of his crisis. The dirty girl is a small replica of the public threatening, suffered for the musician on stage.

The interpretation of the dirty woman as a representation of the spectators is given by multiple images. Pink's car enters a parking lot. Five women come walking behind. A sign warns: "Backstage area. Absolutely not admittance". Women progress to a barrier where is read: "Not Cross". A guard tries to stop them. He can not. Then another also fails in its attempt to stop the fanatical persons. Finally, they reach the caravan of trailers. Seduce the manager and the whole entourage. And finally, one of the fanatical persons reaches to Pink. There is no way to contain the fanatical persons. They ignore all warnings and they mock security systems. The threat is latent. The crisis is inevitable. The theme of fanatical persons without barriers becomes in a recurrent theme. First, it was at the double door, at the fence, and now in the caravan.

Destroyed apartment window

The dirty woman of caravan was not the answer to the question of Pink. It produces, however, a new crisis of panic, the desire to destroy everything. Pink destroys his belongings from the apartment in the trailer. The dirty woman flees fearful of being attacked by Pink. She abandons the trailer of the caravan. Finally, Pink hits the window glasses. He breaks the glass panes. He goes up to the window with the intention of crossing finally across the wall, but meets the vacuum. He is not at three echelons from the ground in front of the entrance to the trailer. Now he is on the top floor of a building. He holds the window frame to avoid falling into the abyss. His foot is swinging dangerously into nothingness. Below, far below, he sees only the asphalt of the street full of cars and in front, rows of tall buildings.

Pink faces another failed attempt to cross the wall. The answer to his question, this time, was the void, the abyss. This output also motivates not cross the wall, if he goes out the window he can fall the abyss. If he go out the door was fall in the crisis. With some disappointment and panic, Pink wobbles in a vacuum, while holding on tightly to the metal frame of the window.

The destroyed TV screen

Anguished and disappointed by the failed attempt to cross the wall through the window, Pink goes into the apartment of the trailer. There continues the destruction of the things. He is pausing for a moment. He sees the TV. Hopeful is directed toward it. Maybe that is the way to cross to the other side of the wall. With his guitar, he hits the screen. It explodes into pieces. Now, it is a black hole. This represents other failed attempt to Pink to cross to the other side of the wall. It is another failed attempt to overcome panic metaphor to fanatical persons. It is another failed attempt to give a different meaning to the symbol interposed between the fanatical persons and the musician on stage. It is another failed attempt to tear down the wall as a symbol, a metaphor for the barrier mocked by fanatical persons. It is another failed attempt to overcome the panic to the fanatical persons out of control.

Pink's question whether, there is anyone outside the wall, other fanatical persons promoters of discord among the public, once again, it is left unanswered. The characters reflected in the screen, are not within the drawer to answer the question. Instead, there is a black hole, nothing. The door leads to the crisis. The window leads to the abyss. The television screen leads to the nothing. Definitely, Pink loses hope. There is no incentive to cross the wall.

Pink gives up. He goes into his autistic personality. The situations, out of order, generates him crisis. He decides to establish his own order of things. He takes objects and ranks them by their shape and size (55:00). With them, he builds the ideal place for an autistic person. Until the pink pills to calm him, they are settled in that autistic space. For the first time, Pink does not feel threatened. His phobia to the fanatics disappears. Now, he seems an innocent child and not a musician in panic at criticism.

The objects for his autistic world are taken of the drawer of the destroyed television. The screen had been broken before with the guitar. At last, the TV is useful for something. It is no longer the means of failed communication, as will be seen later. It is not a contact with the other side of the wall. Now the television set is a provider (55:50). It provides components for the perfect world of Pink.

With his ideal world built, he is ready to bring down his body wall. He opens cracks in his skin, that wall between his organic being and the outside world. The razor blade makes cutting the skin. Pink's blood, his vital essence, crosses to the other side of the wall (56:40).

The free fall in the pool

Pink has tried by various means to find an answer to his question whether "there is someone out there", someone who be different to fanatics, but no response. It has entered the phase of total disappointment. He seems to conclude about the useless of his efforts. There is no way to find an answer to his question beyond the wall. Then, he decides to look in his own wall: the skin. He shaved first the hair and beard. And then, he shaved his chest with lacerations. He opens holes in that wall of separation between inside and outside himself. Perhaps the answer lies in that thin wall between the flesh and the world.

Pink disarms the shaving machine (56:10). He takes the blade. With his thumb and forefinger, he tries of breaking the blade in two. His fingers are cut before they succeed. Pink bleeds. He shaved his eyebrows with lacerations in a clear goodbye to a life without answers, without anything beyond the wall. Of background, the song "Another Brick in the Wall, Part 3" sounds:

I don't need no arms around me

And I don't need no drugs to calm me.

I have seen the writing on the wall.

Don't think I need anything at all.

No! Don't think I'll need anything at all.

All in all it was all just bricks in the wall.

All in all you were all just bricks in the wall.

The lyrics, of the song of background, sounds like a decision, to a full person, to a person with certainty. Pink has seen the writing on the wall. He understood the meaning of the wall. (12:20) Pink is sinking in the pool of his own blood. He drowns in red liquid poured down the wall of his skin. He goes into free fall with the pool water. Inside, he is released with the red jets through the holes in his skin. Pink has decided to abandon this "Cruel World". At last, he has found the answer to his question. Now nothing more can reach him, touch him. Now he feels no anguish at fanatics. Now he feels comfortably numb. He feels in transition to full calm.

The lively shell of doom

After the free fall in the pool, the worms begin their task of decomposing the flesh. Worms are the unmistakable sign of a lifeless body. They only eat dead flesh. It is the final phase towards the total extinction of human beings. They return the meat to dust, to earth. Then, they must face the final judgment about the actions during their existence. Some live this like the light at the end of the tunnel. Pink, however, confronts at a judge worm.

The worm judge called several witnesses, outside observers of the existence of Pink. When the mother asks if she can take his boy back home, Pink floats in the sky. He is a crazy floating in the sky, in the rainbow, says the lyrics of the song. He hits against the animated background and this is broken like a shell. Then, Pink enters floating into a black hole. He has crossed the light at the end of the tunnel and beyond. The judgment did not send him back as in life after death. He must continue his journey to ultimate extinction.

Luis Carlos Molina Acevedo

The wall explodes into pieces

The judgment did not stop the course toward the final extinction of Pink. The worm judge gives his verdict. The wall must be collapsed and the accused exposed to the eyes of everyone, including fanatical persons who created his phobia. Pink loses all chance of beating to death and to come back to life. He should continue his way past the tunnel toward another unknown reality for the living.

When the wall fell, the dead body of Pink is exposed in full view of everyone. He can no longer hide behind any wall, any spittle, any crisis, any abyss, or any black hole. Now, Pink can be observed without that he feels panic, anxiety, or phobia. He can no longer recognize the disorder in his autistic order of world. The question of whether "there is anyone outside the wall", it has not an answer because it is made by an autistic person and not by a crazy person, as it is the trend to believe. So, if a response was given, the interrogator would not understand its meaning, because it would be given from a world with a different order to the order of his world. "Your lips move but I can't hear what you're saying". The wall as a sign itself is the only answer. In the wall is written what is really essential. The wall falls only when existence ends.

Television

Besides the attempts of Pink to cross to the other side of the wall, the film emphasizes two means to communicate with the other side of the wall, not through it. One is TV and the other is the telephone.

Television as a technological medium, in the film acquires the status of a main character. The TV says most dialogues in the film. It is almost the unique in talking during the development of theme. To the TV is granted talking while to Pink no. Through it, the singer has contact with the outside world. It goes through the wall without need cracks, doors, windows. It brings information toward this side of the wall. Its bright screen is a sedative. It has a calming effect. He can feel comfortably numb without need of closing your eyes. The musician has not needed to ask if there is someone on the other side of the wall. They are the most peaceful and calm moments for him when he can sit in front of the television, away from the stages, away from fanatical persons. There are no threats. He can have the gaze ajar of an autistic person, without problems. He can also do drugs in front of the television, uncensored.

As stated earlier, Pink sees on TV an old war movie called "The Dam Busters". It is the biography of Barnes Wallis. He invented the bouncing bomb. The film talks about the war and strategies to bring it to an end. In his dialogues, there is a great influence toward the lyrics of the songs from the soundtrack to film "The Wall". For example, in the meeting of Barnes Wallis with Mutt, there is the following dialogue:

"Are you wondering what all this is and I can not tell you because I myself do not know? But I know it's important and if successful, their results could shorten the duration of this war ..."

The verse "I can not explain, you would not understand," in the song "Comfortably Numb" is quite similar.

The TV dialogues appear in several sequences of the film. The screenwriter was concerned to establish confluences between the dialogues and the themes of the film. For example, when the song "Nobody Home" sounds in the background, it speaks about the black book of poems, while the following dialogue is heard on television:

"Hello, Nigger, old friend. What do you do? Hello, little Nigger. No, not here, boy! Come on."

Nigger on television is the name of the main character's dog. This dialogue denotes friendship between the owner and the dog. It is comparable to friendship the singer with his black book of poems. He can tell to it all the vicissitudes of his soul, without prejudices.

And if there were still doubts about the validity of this interpretation, there is a confluence more. Pink is sitting on the floor next to the toilet in the bathroom. His hands are holding black book of poems. He is humming one of his poems. In this sequence of the film, the following dialog television is heard in the background:

"Nigger quiet. Nigger quiet."

Here the coincidence in no case can be accidental. It is intentional. The dialogue has been repeated to make it converge with the scene about black book in the bathroom.

The death process of Pink, as I have stated elsewhere, begins at the moment when he is injected with adrenaline to wake him of the hallucinogenic trip. At that time, the child and the adult, into Pink, are found in the film. The dialogue on TV is the following:

"Sorry, Mr. It is the little Nigger. It was hit by a car. It is dead. The car is not stopped."

"Where did it happen?"

"In front of the main entrance. He ran across the street, Sr., and the car ran over him."

"Where is?"

"In the guardroom, Sr."

This confluence is fairly important. The dialogue about death of the dog sounds at the same time when Pink has started its journey towards the light at the end of the tunnel. It is a further element to reinforce the validity of the interpretation of the death of Pink, as opposed to the interpretation of most analysts of this film who consider that Pink is not dead, he was transformed in dictator.

The television, in short, gives no arguments to cross to the other side of the wall. Its display shows a grim picture on the other side of the wall. There are fighter planes, pilots, and bombers, there. There are acts of war, one after another, to shorten the duration of the armed conflict. It should increase the amount of bombs dropped. There's only destruction and death. The best friends die helplessly by them. The drivers are neglected and then they escape without repair of the damage caused. They are like the fanatical persons in the concerts.

About television in the film one could do a whole book. To conclude this section, I want to point out how TV is the central element in the mental oasis of Pink. I will discuss this in the section on "The Desire".

The telephone

This device is another technological protagonist of the film, but less than television. Unlike what happens with the television, in the case of telephone, the contact with the other side of the wall always failed. Both point to the problem of communication. From the point of view of an autistic person, the other persons have difficulty expressing their emotions, feelings and thoughts. It is curious to note how these elements are expressed in the starting metaphor for the theme of the film. In the words of its screenwriter, he is forced to spit to the fanatical person next to the stage, because that person was hindering the communication of the group with the spectators.

In the case of television, communication is hindered by the passivity of the viewer. This technological device forces a gaze ajar to create an autistic aura. The viewer is isolated. He watches toward his mental world. From that point on, any attempt to communicate with him it will fail. There is a fail when the wife gets naked and wants sex with Pink. There is a fail when the dirty woman wants to know everything about that place where Pink lives, when she wants to go with him to the tub. There is a fail when manager wants to wake him to go to the concert. There is a fail when the doctor wants to know where it hurts. In the song "Nobody Home", a verse says:

"Got thirteen channels of shit on the T.V. to choose from"

In the case of the telephone, not only the communication fails. It also fails in several attempts to contact the other side of the wall. In this, TV wins. There are three times when the telephone is useless. No one answered the telephone when Pink, touring the United States, wants to talk to his wife. The singer decided to disconnect the device as a sign of its ineffectiveness. In the second attempt, the handset falls from the dead hand of the father of Pink, before asking for help on the other side of the wall, on the other side of the trench. (70: 48) And on the third try, the manager tries to call, but the telephone is disconnected, in the hotel room. This occurs when Pink was dragged toward the concert.

The telephone does contact the other side of the wall three times. After the first attempt of Pink of calling his wife from his hotel, he tries again. A man's voice is heard on the other side of the phone. This takes by surprise to Pink. Still, he asks his wife at the telephone. The voice on the other end says nothing and hangs up. The second time, it occurs from a pay telephone. Pink does a call payable. The operator asks the man on the other side, if he receives a collect call from Mr. Pink from the United States. The man hangs up the telephone without saying anything. The operator says: "It seems that they hung". Without understand the situation, she redials. Hearing the man's voice on the other end says, "There seems to be another man with his wife Mr. Pink ..." The singer let fall the handset, like his father years ago in the trenches. He also falls to the floor with a feel of death in his body. The telephone does not provide the communications as industry touts. In the song "Nobody Home" says:

I've got amazing powers of observation.

And that is how I know

When I try to get through

On the telephone to you

There will be nobody home...

Ooooh, Babe when I pick up the phone

There's still nobody home.

The telephone tells him, from the other side of the wall, only bad things. Another man is in bed beside his wife. The wife is gone, without warning. Here's another reason for not wanting to know anything about the other side of the wall.

THE REAL

The real facts of the movie "Pink Floyd The Wall" last a very short time. It runs from the time when it begins to sound the theme of Santa Claus (00:12), with the image of the hotel corridor, while the camera moves forward, until the moment when Pink died in the back seat of the limousine in way toward the concert. Between the beginning and the end, the cleaning employee tries to open the room door of Pink (5:35). As she can not do it and she receives not response, she reports the situation to direction. They should force the door to enter. The manager comes with some employees of the caravan, the hotel manager, and two paramedics (66:15). A doctor injects to Pink to revive him. He is dressed for the concert by two men, still without awakening. Two men dragged him out of the hotel room. They take him through the corridor. They go down by the stairs. They take him to the limo. They let on him in the back seat. Pink dies in way to the concert.

This stage consists of several sequences interspersed at different points of the film. The camera continues to move down the hall, almost to the end. In the background, a cleaning employee takes out the vacuum cleaner from one of the rooms (0030). She left it in the corridor and she goes back to the room. When back out again, she switches on the vacuum cleaner. Film credits appear.

The sound of the vacuum cleaner, before showing to the cleaning employee is heard. She switches off the vacuum cleaner and goes to the room door of Pink. She taps several times. Nobody opens. She seeks her key to open. The chain is shaken. The manager of tour appears with the hotel manager, two paramedics and members of the entourage of the tour. They try to revive to Pink. He is injected by the medic. They dragged him out toward the limo. They sit him in the back seat. Pink is devoured by worms. Literally, at this point, the facts of the film end. The remaining sequences are memories, imaginations and desires.

The real facts of the film last nine minutes and six seconds, as follows:

First sequence occurs in the hallway with the cleaning employee, from (00:15) to (01:37), one minute and 22 seconds long.

The second sequence occurs between the cleaning employee in the corridor and Pink in the room, from (4:15) to (5:51), one minute and 31 seconds long.

The third sequence occurs between the entrance of the manager into the hotel room and the transformation of Pink in dictator on the back seat of the limousine, from (66:15) to (72:25), six minutes and 10 seconds long.

Is There Anybody Out The Wall?

The lever of the real for mental travel in time by Pink has four stages:

1. The hotel corridor (00:15)

2. The hotel room (66:15)

3. The emergency staircase (71:15)

4. The limo toward the concert (71:58)

Other scenes, into hotel, correspond with the mental world of Pink's memories. These events occur within the apartment of the caravan for concert tour. The film as is shown by the facts, only covers the cleaning employee; Pink with a burned cigar between his fingers in the hotel room; the manager into the hotel room; Pink dragged through the hotel lobby and stairs until the limousine.

The hotel corridor

The film begins with a sequence of a hotel corridor and a cleaning employee in it is shown (00:12). In the background the song "The Little Boy That Santa Claus Forgot" by Vera Lynn sounds:

Christmas comes for all children (01:00)

Laughter and joy

It is in every new toy.

I'll tell you about a little boy who lives near here

For this boy Christmas is just another day.

The cleaning employee switches on the vacuum cleaner and then they are shown the credits of film (1:38). When the credits finish, two sequences occur, one carried by the lever of the imagination (the father of Pink preparing to go to war 02:00), and the other carried by lever of the memories (Little Pink runs in an open field towards the encounter with the adult Pink 3:54). Then, the camera returns to the hotel corridor. The song of Santa Claus keeps sounding:

(4:15) He is the boy that Santa Claus forgot.

And God knows I did not ask for much

He sent a letter to Santa.

He wanted some soldiers and a drum

His little heart broke when I saw that Santa did not come

Outside was envious of those lucky children.

After showing to Pink in the interior of the room (04:15), the camera returns to the image of the cleaning employee (05:00). She turns off the vacuum cleaner. She addresses the room door of Pink. She calls. The face of Pink is shown and then, the security chain on the door of the hotel room, it is zoomed. The cleaning employee takes his keys to open (05:35). The chained door is to be shaken. Then, it is changed to another sequence of images carried by the lever of the imagination.

The hotel room

While the song of Santa Claus is sounded, the image sequence changes from the hotel corridor to a close up of a clock with the image of Mickey Mouse (04:15). The camera moves along the left arm to take the image of burned cigarette. And then, it makes a zoom toward the face of Pink. The zoom keeps toward the right eye and simulates go to inner of him. The theme of the film is indicated, from now, to the spectator. It is a mental journey of the musician toward different moments of his life.

After several sequences carried by the levers of imagination, memories and desire, it turns to activate the lever to travel on the real. The wall to be collapsed is shown for the first time. Then, the image of burned cigarette of marijuana between the fingers of Pink is shown. The camera is rolling along the left arm of Pink and it keeps until focusing on his face. He is staring at the TV. Image of the wall is then inserted again.

After several sequences activated by other levers, it becomes to the time line of reality. Pink is asleep in the chair in front of the television. The door is pushed to be opened. The door opens and the tour manager appears who says:

"Fuck me."

"He's gone completely around the bleedin' twist."

"You vicious bastard, you never did like me, did you?"

"And get you on your feet again", says the hotel manager.

The lyric of the song asks:

Is there anyone out there?

Is there anyone out there?

Is there anyone out there…?

Other song continues:

Hello, is there anybody in there?

Just nod if you can hear me.

Is there anyone at home?

Come on, now, I hear you're feeling down.

Well I can ease your pain

Get you on your feet again.

Relax, I'll need some information first.

Just the basic facts.

Can you show me where it hurts?

There is no pain you are receding

A distant ship, smoke on the horizon.

You are only coming through in waves.

Your lips move but I can't hear what you're saying.

When I was a child I had a fever

Is There Anybody Out The Wall?

My hands felt just like two balloons.

Now I've got that feeling once again

I can't explain, you would not understand

This is not how I am.

I have become comfortably numb.

Ok, just a little pinprick.

There'll be no more aaaaaaaaah!

But you may feel a little sick.

Can you stand up?

I do believe it's working, good.

That'll keep you going through the show

Come on it's time to go.

There is no pain you are receding

A distant ship, smoke on the horizon.

You are only coming through in waves.

Your lips move but I can't hear what you're saying.

When I was a child I caught a fleeting glimpse

Out of the corner of my eye.

I turned to look but it was gone

I cannot put my finger on it now

The child is grown, the dream is gone.

I have become comfortably numb.

While "Comfortably Numb" sounds in the background, the entourage of the tour manager examines the eyes of Pink. An oxygen mask is set to Pink's face and he is deposited on a stretcher by paramedics. The tour manager says:

"The boy's an asthmatic", says the manager of the tour.

"Asthmatic!?" asks the hotel manager

"Relax"

"I'll need some information first."

"He's an artist!"

"Good"

At this point a sequence is introduced, activated by the lever of memories. The sequence is repeated four times in the film (3:54, 53:27, 62:03, and 67:15). It shows an open field with a rugby bow at the background. In three of the four times, a silhouette of a person backlit moves towards the camera and then, it switches to another sequence. This time, the silhouette comes enough close up to the camera to reveal who is (67:15). It is Pinky. Little Pink keeps moving in the open field. He finds a sick rat. The boy takes it in his hands. He returns home with her. The lyric of the song says:

"As a child I had a fever"

The verses are to be converged with the images to tell to the spectator about the disease of rat. But it is also the deadly disease of Pink. Although rugby pitch sequence is repeated four times, the tonality of colours is different to indicate the different moments of the existence of Pink. When the time line of film is on 53 minutes and 27 seconds, the musician says goodbye to this cruel world. The field has orange hue, indicating the declination of life (53:27). The sun is in the west. In the first appearance of the sequence, the sun is rising (3:54). It indicates the beginning of the life of Pink. And in the last occurrence of the sequence, the sun does not illuminate the field, it's the moon. It indicates the income of Pink in the other world, on the other side of the wall, in death.

The mother works in the sewing machine. Pinky has the rat among his hands. He offers it to the mother. She gets up from her chair horrified. The child runs out with the rat. It is inserted again the sequence of Pinky with fever.

The camera changes to the image of Pink on the stretcher and the manager trying to wake him. A doctor injects to Pink. They hope to awaken the singer but it converts the numbness, until this point, in a journey toward death. The injection of adrenaline sent to musician toward a trip by the tunnel of light. The boatman of death will not cross to Pink toward the other side of the river, but a smoky boat, more in line with today's technological age. It is inserted for the first time the image of worms, devouring the flesh. Pink has started to die.

"He's coming around", says the manager of the tour

"That'll keep you going through the show"

"There, you see?"

"Come on, it's time to go"

"How do you feel?"

The sequence shows to Pinky now walking back to the room of St. Alexius to review the rat. It is dead (69:45). He strips it to the river. He sees how it sinks into the water. He is also sinking in the pool of his own blood. He is also dying. He is also being devoured by worms, like they now do with the rat. He is another rat dying, a being negligible. Now it is a being depreciated by his mother too.

The rat is a symbol of death without return. The water carries it far away, like now he is transported by a distant ship, smoke on the horizon. Both are carried by the boatman of death to the other side of the river. The rat, as symbol of death, appears three times in the film. The first, when starting the film, the camera displays the clock of Pink with image of Mickey Mouse. At that time, the narcotic intoxication begins to numb to Pink watching television. The second time, occurs when Pink finds the sick rat in the open field. And the third time, occurs when the mother sees to Pink in the coffin. Her hairstyle makes her look like Mickey Mouse.

The wake begins. The father looks at him through the glass of the coffin (69:30). He brings the dead rat hanging by tail. Then, it begins the accompaniment toward the grave. Only the dead persons come to his funeral. They parade by the place fenced with barbed wire and hammers as field stakes. It is another form of the wall. By there, the dead father goes with the rat hanging on the tip of his tail between his index finger and thumb of the right hand. The dead persons help him to cross to the other side of the wall. On the fenced field also parade the professor, the doctor of childhood (British doctor), and dead soldiers. The only live person, from this side of the wall, who sees him dead, it is his mother. She also looks at him smiling through the coffin glass. Her hair gives to her a look similar to the face of Mickey Mouse. She kisses the glass and then she keeps going long (68:22). She sees him in the coffin, but not in the field of the wake. Only dead persons can march by that place. The medic of childhood, now dead, also sees him into the coffin. He shows to Pink, through the glass, a syringe, just before he receives the injection of the doctor in the hotel room. Then, the father shows him the dead rat through the coffin glass (69:32). That is the ultimate death.

Two men, from the retinue of the manager, straighten to Pink in his chair after injection. They put off the shirt of the singer (70:15). With him without force and his eyes closed in the process of death, they begin to dress him for the show. Upon completion of dressing him, they raise him from the chair. They dragged him out of the room.

Emergency stairs

The two men drag to Pink by the hotel hallway (70:55). Pink's left hand is eaten by the worms, his whole body too. They arrive at the hotel emergency staircase. They must get out him by the back door. No one should see to Pink in that state. They descend by it with difficulty. Meanwhile, several image sequences are interspersed which they are activated with other levers of the mental machine to travel in time. Several sequences of images about worms are interspersed to indicate the death process lived by Pink at that time (71:05, 71:20, 71:30, and 71:45).

The two men, with Pink nearly dead, come to the end of the corridor. They begin the descent by the endless metal ladders. In a kind of basement, the limo is waiting by them. They open the back door and sit to Pink in the seat (71:55).

Luis Carlos Molina Acevedo

The limousine

The camera shows to Pink in the back seat of the limousine. The singer is now a blur mass of flesh eaten by worms (72:00). The dying process has come to an end. The musician is ready for final judgment. Old Pink disappears between pieces of wormy flesh torn from his body with his own hands. The whole mass of meat, eaten by worms, disappears. In his place, a new Pink appears. Now he is dressed like a dictator (72:25).

The skinhead is ready for the concert (72:36). His face was revitalized. The uniform of dictator makes him appear stronger. But this character is another fantasy of Pink who just died. It is a sequence activated by the lever of the desire in his mental machine to travel in time.

Luis Carlos Molina Acevedo

THE MEMORY

The memories are a lever of the mental machine to travel in time, with which Pink can return to his childhood. The memories of the singer are shown in six scenes:

1. With the mother (12:51)

2. At school (23:04)

3. With Friends (21:14)

4. At Home (15:56)

5. In the park (14:04)

6. In the ballroom (34:03)

Luis Carlos Molina Acevedo

With the mother

There is a sequence, in the film, which is shown as if it was a memory of Pink, but it really is a sequence activated by the lever of the imagination. It is the scene about the mother sleeping in the garden and little Pink crying into the white baby carriage. This scene is recreated by the imagination of the musician. He can not have a memory of this time. From his baby carriage, he could not see the garden and his mother sleeping.

The first real memory of Pink, in the film, it is when the mother prays in the church (13:00). Pink plays with a pennant. Then, the camera shows him playing with a small fighter plane on a railing. Occasionally he looks up to look at his mother, who keeps on his knees before the altar. He only sees her back. The mother weeps silently. In the background sounds the song "Another Brick in the Wall, Part 1":

Daddy's flown across the ocean

Leaving just a memory

A snapshot in the family album

Daddy what else did you leave for me?

Daddy, what d'ya leave behind for me?

Luis Carlos Molina Acevedo

All in all it was just a brick in the wall.

All in all it was all just bricks in the wall.

A marble appears with the inscription "1939-1945 in honour of the officers, non-commissioned officers and men of the 8th/9th Battalion, the Royal united who gave their lives in the Second World War at Anzio A.D. 1944". Then, it switches to a sequence where the mother leaves her son at the park.

Another memory of Pinky about his mother, it is when he sleeps in her arms. There is a direct reference to the over protection of the mother for her child. Here, over protection takes also the meaning of death. There is a fear of the mother to lose her son the same way as lost her husband. This meaning does not escape to the mind of the little Pinky. At night, he gets up scared and runs to her mother's bed. He aspires to sleep in the arms of his mother again. Opening the door, he can not help to express disappointment. Her mother already has company. She is sleeping beside the skeleton of her husband. The small finds that behind the affection of his mother toward him, there is not a true filial love, but the projection of her inner fear. That fills him of doubts towards life. That takes him to ask existential questions to his mother, as reflected in the song "Mother". This song includes the four questions about the existence, projected by Pink, and here formulated as the four levers of mental machine to travel back in time.

At school

After the scene of the train in the tunnel, Pinky hears the teacher's voice in his mind. The camera switches to the school scene. The teacher appears in the image, while saying:

"You!"

"You! Yes, you!"

"Stand still, laddie!"

In the Background sounds the song "The Happiest Days of Our Lives":

When we grew up and went to school
There were certain teachers who would
Hurt the children in any way they could
By pouring their derision upon anything we did
And exposing every weakness
However carefully hidden by the kids
But in the town, it was well known
When they got home at night, their fat and
Psychopathic wives would thrash them
Within inches of their lives.

The camera shows the teacher asking questions to Pinky, after taking a sheet of paper from the desk of him, he says:

"What have we here, laddie? Mysterious scribblings? A secret code? No. Poems, no less. Poems, everybody! The lad here reckons himself a poet. 'Money, get back. I'm all right, Jack. Keep your hands off my stack. New car, caviar, four-star daydream. Think I'll buy me a football team'. Absolute rubbish, laddie! Get on with your work."

The poem is destroyed by the teacher. It is the content of the song "Money".

The teacher returns to his class. He turns his back to Pinky and he wanders around the classroom, while forcing students to repeat his explanations:

"Repeat after me: An acre is the area of a rectangle whose length is one furlong and whose width is one chain."

"Wrong! Do it again! An acre is the area of a rectangle whose length is one furlong and whose width is one chain."

This sequence wants to show the no education provided at school. Contrary to the findings at first glance, the film does not reject education, but the no education. That is, it rejects the rote education, the dark sarcasm, the exposition of the weaknesses of the student.

We don't need no education.

This verse is repeated several times in the song "Another Brick in the Wall, Part 2". The use of the double negation, in the logical sense, becomes an affirmation. There is a yes to education, but a different education from current.

We don't need no thought control.

This verse is also repeated in this song. Here, through the same process of double negation, it is obtained an affirmation. That is, it wants the thought control, but maybe a control to reach a most exemplary life for the human being. Here, again, it reflects the autistic personality of Pink, of the dictator. It is a singer with the need for an orderly world, without criticism.

Luis Carlos Molina Acevedo

With friends

In the movie, the little Pink does not seem to have many friends. Only it appears in a scene with two. He runs with them through a hill.

"Wait for me, Pinky, you rotten bleeder."

"They're my bullets, ain't they?"

"I don't know."

"Come on, Tubs. It's great down in the tunnel."

"Don't you think it'd be dangerous, Pinky?"

"No. Don't be daft."

"You all right, Tubs?"

"Yeah. Hurt me knee a bit."

This dialogue seems to denote a single friend of the little Pink. It is the only one who is called by his own name. Pinky takes the bullets of the box and delivers them to their peers.

"Como on."

"Na. It's too dangerous."

"We'll wait for the train."

"Give me the torch."

In the tunnel, the bullet is exploded by train. Then, several hands dangle through the windows of the wagons. Then, they emerge blurry faces. Everyone seems blame to Pinky for their suffering. The boy hears the teacher's voice in his head. He censures him by his conduct.

In the House

Little Pink comes home from school. He searches something of marmalade. He smears it on the bread. He goes up the stairs toward the top floor of the house. He sees the open door of the marital bedroom. He is returned. He checks if the mother is there. No this. He enters. He opens the dresser drawers. One contains the underwear of the mother. Other contains the objects of his dead father. In the background sounds the song "When the Tigers Broke Free, part 2":

And kind old King George sent Mother a note

When he heard that Father was gone.

It was, I recall, in the form of a scroll,

With gold leaf and all.

And I found it one day

In a drawer of old photographs, hidden away.

And my eyes still grow damp to remember

His Majesty signed with his own rubber stamp.

It was dark all around, there was frost in the ground

When the Tigers broke free.

And no one survived

From the Royal Fusiliers Company C.
They were all left behind,
Most of them dead, the rest of them dying.
And that's how the High Command
Took my daddy from me.

The camera shows a sequence of images where the little Pink put on the kepi of his father. Then, he takes the parchment and he opens it. Then he takes the razor. After that, he opens the box of bullets. He dresses the uniform of his father. He looks himself in the mirror. He imagines how his father would look with that uniform.

And finally, another memory of Pink in the house is when he is sick. He studies in his room. Suddenly, he sees his neighbour in front, undressing in her room. He turns off the light to observe without being seen. The mother enters to the room and he should dissemble. The woman finds her son with fever. She calls the doctor. The mother worries. Think of the possible loss of her boy too. The doctor says no problem. It's nothing serious. It is only the fever of adolescence. It is the hormonal changes in their apogee. The mother, embarrassed, hurries to close the door. The boy should not hear the doctor's explanation. But the teen deducts, from the behaviour of the mother, the severity of his health.

In the park

The other places in the memory of Pink are the park, and the ballroom.

The mother leaves him at the park. Pinky roams the place. When he sees a man playing with his granddaughter, he walked toward him. Man makes spinning the carousel with her granddaughter on it while he tells her:

"Easy. Be careful."

"What?" asks man.

"Will you put me on there?" asks Pinky.

"Well, where's your mother, then?" asks man.

"She's gone to the shops" says Pinky.

"Yes, all right."

"How's that then? Enjoying it?" asks man.

"Lovely, lovely" says man.

"Now off you go. Go on."

"Now what have I told you about this? What have I told you? Go on, go on now. Sling your hook. Go on. Sling your hook."

Pinky is forced to release the man's arm. He sees the man goes away from the park with her granddaughter. He sits alone on a swing. He tries of pushing himself and can not. His gaze discovers other children on swings, driven by their parents.

This scene leads to Pink to take awareness about the absence of his father, not like a fact itself, but by a deduction process. He really did not know his father. He can not know what the lack of a father is. This becomes evident for him by the ordering of society. By it, he is forced to feel a lack like this. The earliest memory of Pinky is about the church, where the mother prayed. She leaves him in the park and goes to do her shopping. There, the boy discovers the absence of his father. There is no one who to push him on the swings. No one takes him by the hand to go home. It is society that makes him feel the need for a father. Pink's father really dies in the park. There are others who with their questions showed him the lack of a father: What does your father do? What is the name of your dad...?

In the park, Pinky discovered the absence of his father. Therefore, this place occupies an important position in the lever to travel to the past. At that time, his father really dies, and not before. At that moment he becomes aware of the meaning of the word "father".

In the ballroom

The other space in the memory of Pink is the ballroom. Everyone dances, while Pinky is sitting alone in a chair. After a while, he decides to get up and cross to the other side of the room, by between couples. There, he meets a girl. She is also sitting alone in a chair. He invites her to dance. She is taller than him. This is indicative of more old too. From the context of the film, one can follow this girl later became the wife of Pink. It's the same girl of the window in front at his house.

In the ballroom, Pink met who would be his future wife. For that, this place has a high importance in the memories of the singer. Two lonely join their lives with the hope to be a companion for the other. But in reality, they are still two solitary people, even at the moment of sex.

Luis Carlos Molina Acevedo

THE IMAGINATION

The lever of imagination allows travel through time possible, potential. It consists of all moments non witnessed by Pink, but created by him as part of his mental world. Here, it is vital the artistic creation, reflected through the animated images in the film. But the re-creation of moments narrated by others is not the only function of artistic creation. With it, the musician can also express their truths and opinions indirectly. In the film one can identify four scenes of the imagination:

1. The father in the war (08:22)

2. Childhood before conscious memories (9:08)

3. Infidelity of his wife (35:11)

4. The animated expression of various concepts

Luis Carlos Molina Acevedo

The father in the war

The first activation of the lever to travel on the potential time into the world of imagination, it is represented by sequence of the father of Pink and his preparation for going to war. Pink never knew his father, but he can imagine the important moments in life of him. He knows about him, what was said by others, what was said by the hidden objects in a dresser in the marital bedroom. With these elements he can imagine how his father was then, before going to war. The father lit a match in the dark to take existence. With it, he lights a lamp. Then he lights a cigarette. While smoking, he cleans his gun.

With his imagination, he follows the father in the war. He explores the world of explosions, shelling. Planes fly like birds, like crosses, before dropping the bombs. The soldiers are killed. Others are injured. They are collected as if they were garbage left by the war. The images re-create the cruelty of the military conflict.

The lever of imagination takes us now to the time of death of the father. The plane is close. The father sees it coming. He ran toward the telephone to call for help to the Central Command. The bomb exploded before dialling the number. The body of soldier slides into the floor with the headphone in his hand. Then, life is permanently discontinued, the hand releases the headphone. It swings through the air like a pendulum. It marks the end of that time there. At the mental world of the imagination, a child is left without a father.

Pinky is now in the matrimonial bedroom. He takes from the dresser drawer, things of his father. He put on the kepi. Then, he dons the uniform. He looks himself at the mirror. Through his reflection, he can imagine the look of his father with that uniform. The sequence makes several transitions between Pinky and the image of his father in the mirror.

Imagination also allows to Pink to see his father become skeleton, in the same marriage bedroom. The skeleton was sleeping next to his mother. Perhaps it is the memory of the moment when the remains of the dead father was removed. This is suggested by the hair of the skull.

With the imagination, Pink also re-creates the wake of his death. It is attended by all the dead with some presence in his life. The parade is begun by the father with the rat hanging on the tip of the tail, in his right hand. It follows the school teacher. Then, the doctor of childhood goes. Behind they are other dead soldiers; perhaps they are family of Pink. "After all it was just bricks in the wall." All persons march by the place with barbed wire and poles hammer-shaped field.

Imagined childhood

The mother sleeps in a rocking chair in the garden. Little Pink cries (09:15). He is in the baby white carriage on the other side of the garden.

The previous scene is repeated (19:00). This time, the camera makes a panning from the baby crying to a cat in the grass. The cat has a concentrated gaze. The animal waits the moment to attack. When it does, a white dove flies to escape the cat.

Luis Carlos Molina Acevedo

The unfaithful wife

Wife infidelity is another scene of the imaginary world of Pink. He was not present in the scene, because he was on tour in the United States, but he imagines it. The camera captures an expositor. He is speaking before an audience about peace. When the spectator wonders about the meaning of that scene in the film, the camera takes the wife of Pink, sitting in the audience. The spectator organized his papers. The wife keeps sitting in the same chair. The others are gone. The wife drinking with the expositor in a public place is then displayed. After that, the two are in bed, naked, half covered by sheets. The telephone rings. The man attends and hangs up.

Wife infidelity, takes on great significance in the existence of Pink. He will feel cheated, abandoned. Perhaps no love, but he got used to her. He needs her. The lyrics of the song "Do not Leave Me Now" talks about that experience.

Luis Carlos Molina Acevedo

Animated concepts

It is shown a cat in the grass (19:00). His gaze is of concentration. The cat waits the moment to attack. When it does, a white dove flies to escape the cat. The dove rises into the air. The bird becomes animated pigeon. It becomes a black cartoon bird. It explodes in blood and emerges a black eagle. It flies over the map of a city. It lifts between its claws a sector of houses, leaving a trail of blood. As it rises to heaven, blood drops falls from its clutches. It leaves behind to a monster of luminous eyes. The monster becomes a fleet of warplanes. Beings with biochemical warfare masks are shown.

The planes become crosses. A skeleton falls. England flag is shown. It breaks down into its components. They fall to the ground. Now it is a bleeding cross. The blood slides to the ground. The skeleton has military uniform. From a bone structure, a white dove tries to emerge. Five skeletons, in military dress, advance each behind a cross. The dove flies between them. The cross appears blooding. Blood runs across the floor to a sewer.

Luis Carlos Molina Acevedo

This sequence may suggest many interpretations, from an unpatriotic spirit to a national collapse. In the background sounds the song "Goodbye Blue Sky". His poetry can contribute elements for the interpretation:

Did you see the frightened ones?

Did you hear the falling bombs?

Did you ever wonder why we

Had to run for shelter when the

Promise of a brave, new world

Unfurled beneath the clear blue sky?

Did you see the frightened ones?

Did you hear the falling bombs?

The flames are all long gone, but the pain lingers on.

Goodbye, blue sky

Goodbye, blue sky.

Goodbye. Goodbye.

This sequence re-creates images of despair after the war. The war does not end when it is signed a peace agreement. The aftermath of war remain for many years. "The flames were extinguished in a while but the pain still persists."

Another concept re-created in images, is the relationship between persons. Two animated flowers are shown. The rose is paired with the female flower. It takes shape of a woman from the hips to the feet, faceless. Two white doves fly. The female flower is transfigured, now it is a harpy. It has become carnivorous flower. It devours the male pink. Then, it

92

becomes a black bird in a dark sky filled with clouds. The interpretation, here, seems obvious.

Then, it is recreated the concept of consumption with images. On an open field, a building emerges. The first building appears to fill the empty space. It is multiplied to form the wall. Now, the wall encloses the city full of cars. The flower stem is a barbed wire. A baby grows up to become ape. Then, it becomes a beast. He bats a man. He breaks him the head. Pain faces emerge from the bricks. Notre Dame Church appears. The wall continues to spread. The wall destroys the church to follow its spreading. A luminous frontage appears instead; perhaps it is a place of nightlife. A monstrous figure appears. It is transformed into a creature with a big mouth. From his throat emerges a steam with a way of white dove. Then, it has become in a female body, faceless. The faceless woman is now a strawberry cake and cherries flying. The faceless woman regains form. The woman turns in a machine gun. The machine gun turns in an electric guitar. The guitar becomes in a car. In the background sounds the song "What Shall We Do Now?"

What shall we use to fill the empty spaces

Where waves of hunger roar?

Shall we set out across the sea of faces

In search of more and more applause?

Shall we buy a new guitar?

Shall we drive a more powerful car?

Shall we work straight through the night?

Shall we get into fights?

Leave the lights on? Drop bombs?
Do tours of the east? Contract diseases?
Bury bones? Break up homes?
Send flowers by phone?
Take to drink? Go to shrinks?
Give up meat? Rarely sleep?
Keep people as pets?
Train dogs? Race rats?
Fill the attic with cash?
Bury treasure? Store up leisure?
But never relax at all
With our backs to the wall.

This sequence is a critique of modern life. The consumer society builds walls everywhere in the false belief fill the empty spaces of the existence. But the gap is increasing because what really matters has remained outside the walls: "Could rest with our backs to the wall". We sold our inner calm in exchange for the apparent comfort of modern life stifling, full of empty things. The spaces are not those empty, but the things into a society which forgets what is the truly essential for humans. Even, the woman is sold by advertising as object of desire, it is a faceless being. It is a being with breasts, hips and legs, nothing else matters. It is better if it is commercialized a brainless woman. She is an empty thing.

A hammer emerges from the floor. It is taken by the arm of a man. He breaks a commercial showcase. Man appears in balaclavas. Several looters take those objects exhibited in the shop window. The police arrive. The looters are in confrontation with police. It is the flip side of the consumption. When there is no purchasing power in a consumer society, looting becomes a vital necessity.

The concept of war receives the most criticism through animated images. White doves of peace are transformed into birds of prey. Birds of prey are transfigured in warplanes to drop bombs against humanity. The planes are transfigured in death crosses. The crosses fly. They dig into land where life is extinguished. The flag of Great Britain crumbles. Its components leave the form and they are watered on the floor like dead fallen in war. Now, the flag is a cross of death. She also bleeds with agony. The blood slides to the ground. It runs like rivers of death. It is discarded down the drain like stinking manure. National identity has been evacuated to the sewer of war. "And that's how the High Command took my daddy me". The patriotism has been betrayed by broken promises of rulers. "And my eyes are clouded, remembering that His Majesty signed with his own rubber stamp."

Another concept illustrated with animated images is the final judgment. When Pink is devoured by worms, he is sent before a judge worm. The judge must determine if Pink is guilty of having built a wall or not. Worms are intertwined to form the structure of the court. After, they intertwined with several skulls and form the basket for the big snake Boa. The judge begins the trial. He calls, as a first witness, to the teacher. The teacher appears as a puppet moved by invisible threads, evidenced by the projected shadow on the wall.

In the final judgment, Pink has a skull by head. Again, the camera zooms the right eye socket, as it did at the beginning of the film when Pink appears drugged in front of the television. From it emerges a leaf. It floats in the air to become in Pink, like an inflated doll without facial features. The doll recovers the leaf shape again. It disappears when the camera returns to Pink, sitting on the floor. Beside from him, a snake rises. It becomes scorpion. He spurs to the musician. Now the scorpion takes the form of his wife. She is the second witness in this judgment.

The wall is pierced by an airplane. It flies following the line of the wall. It is transformed into the face of the mother of Pink. She is the third witness in this trial. She takes to Pink in her arms. These become a wall. They leave him again on the floor to continue the trial. Pink floats back into the air like inflated doll. He is floating in the sky. He crashes against the sky and this is broken like a shell. Pink enters the black hole opened in the sky, floats until to be lost in the dark.

The image of a worm is displayed. The upper end takes the form of the head of the worm judge. He begins to give its verdict.

THE DESIRE

With the mental lever of desire to travel in time, Pink goes to the future. The subject is separated from his object of desire by the time between the present and the time to come. This mental space is formed by the duty be of the things, according to Pink. Here, it takes place all his ideas about how the world should be. If sufficient time is desired, the subject reaches its object of desire at the end. The desire of Pink is expressed in the following scenarios:

1. Marriage (32:12)

2. The World

3. Pleasure

4. Mental oasis

5. The Dictator

Luis Carlos Molina Acevedo

Marriage

Pink's marriage, it is a social agreement for a mutual accompaniment. This should last in time despite the difficulties. The musician met his future wife in a ballroom. He, a lonely person, dances with a lonely woman who is greater in age and height. They marry before a notary. When they leave the registry, it's raining. Pink is smiling next to his wife. Something draws the eye of the artist. The expression on his face changed, from a smiling to another of concern. On the floor, tiny red petals are carried by the rain water until the drain. It is similar to blood (32:25). The blood in the drain, it was a bad omen for Britain in the war and now it is also a bad omen for his marriage.

That is a harbinger about future of Pink. His marriage will be painful. He always waited that the protection of his mother could help him, even in that. She should be the filter for the women in his life. She should choose the appropriate one. It was not a matter about love, but of convenience.

Luis Carlos Molina Acevedo

The world

But, what wants Pink? He aspires to an orderly world without wars. A world where politicians, notwithstanding, keep their promises. His desire for a future world, it is reflected in the questions asked to the mother. In the song "Mother", he asks:

Mother do you think they'll drop the bomb?

Mother do you think they'll like this song?

Mother do you think they'll try to break my balls?

Mother should I build the wall?

Mother should I run for president?

Mother should I trust the government?

Mother will they put me in the firing line?

Oooooh Is it just a waste of time?

(Oooooh Mother am I really dying?)

Hush now baby, baby, don't you cry.

Mother's gonna make all your nightmares come true.

Mother's gonna put all of her fears into you.

Mother's gonna keep you right here under her wing.

She won't let you fly, but she might let you sing.

Mama will keep baby cozy and warm.

Ooooh baby ooooh baby oooooh baby,

Of course mama's gonna help build the wall.

Mother do you think she's good enough ... for me?

Mother do you think she's dangerous ... to me?

Mother will she tear your little boy apart?

Mother will she break my heart?

Hush now baby, baby don't you cry.

Mama's gonna check out all your girlfriends for you.

Mama won't let anyone dirty get through.

Mama's gonna wait up until you get in.

Mama will always find out where you've been.

Mama's gonna keep baby healthy and clean.

Ooooh baby oooh baby oooh baby,

You'll always be baby to me.

Mother, did it need to be so high?

This questionnaire is the idea expressed by Pink about ideal world. Even for him, children should not grow, "Mother, did it need to be so high?" Or maybe he should not have been successful.

Pleasure

When Pink is teenager, he faces his desire for women. He studies in the room. In the front window, the neighbour woman is undressing. He turns off the light to see without being seen. The neighbour will be his future wife. The mother enters the room and he should hide his desire.

Pink, in bed, touches shoulder his wife with desire. She turns to the other side.

Pink is in bed watching television. The wife comes home from work. She strips to seduce Pink. He keeps with the eyes on television. She tries to interpose in the visual. But, he moves his head to keep with his eyes on television. She does not insist more and comes out disappointed.

In the caravan of the concert tour, Pink is seeking a dirty woman. She begins to ask questions without stop. The autistic crisis of Pink is triggered. He destroys the things of apartment. The dirty woman is scared. She is afraid of being attacked. A time again, he should postpone his intention of surrendering to pleasure. The lyric, of the song "Young Lust", expresses this intention:

I am just a new boy,

Stranger in this town.

Where are all the good times?

Who's gonna show this stranger around?

Ooooh, I need a dirty woman.

Ooooh, I need a dirty girl.

Will some woman in this desert land

Make me feel like a real man?

Take this rock and roll refugee

Oooh, baby set me free.

Ooooh, I need a dirty woman.

Ooooh, I need a dirty girl.

The pleasure for Pink is an object postponed again and again on the time. But, he stands firm his desire to achieve it someday. The subject and the object of desire are only separate by the time to come, the future. On this, it is based hope of Pink, his decision to go on living, despite adversity. He must only persist and eventually, the time will bring what it is desired.

Mental oasis

This, perhaps, is the genuine desire of Pink. It is taken from the minimalist theory, when it had not been even formulated. It is the existential minimum required: a lamp, a chair, and of course, a TV. The singer does not seem to need anything else in his life. The first image of the mental oasis occurs on the apartment, just after he has destroyed everything (50:15). It is a significant element, the fact of having destroyed, more emphatically, everything that could produce reflections. Pink breaks the mirrors, the framed pictures. He does not want to see his image reflected at all. The room is empty. In one corner, Pink is sitting watching television. Beside him, there is a lamp.

The mental oasis is only possible when he discovers the great truth. Everything that has hitherto been regarded as necessities, were just bricks in the wall. The wall, to be collapsed, becomes more evident at this point in the film (52:40). When removing all the bricks of the wall, it emerges the mental oasis, the existential minimum: a lamp, a chair and a television. Those are the real needs of Pink, anything more, it is a brick added to the wall.

The second appearance of the mental oasis of Pink, it occurs in the open field (59:25). On the foreground, the path fenced with barbed wire and hammer-shaped poles is shown. This is the space of the wake. In the background, one can see to Pink. He is sitting in his mental oasis. The musician writhes in pain. He bends and straightens in his chair by several times. He is transformed into the little Pink (59:50). The child gets up and walks. Pinky enters the path of the wake. He walks by there like a dead person. Look at the skulls in the dust in its wake. Here, then, he will be visited during the wake by the dead persons related with his existence. Among some branches, he discovers an entry. He enters for it. It is a dark room. He walks down a hallway. He enters a gallery of hospital beds. The place is lonely. On a bed, he sees a straitjacket for crazy persons.

Pinky goes into another room and there, he sees to Pink adult, huddled in a corner with his black book of poems between his hands. It is the first and only meeting of child Pink with adult Pink in the film (61:43). It occurs just when Pink is agonizing. Pinky touches to Pink. Pink screams like crazy. Pinky comes out the sanatorium. Now, he runs by the rugby field (62:03). At this time, adult Pink is dying. The encounter with Pinky is part of the journey towards the light at the end of the tunnel.

And the third appearance of the mental oasis of Pink, it takes place in the station of trains (65:49). After the unfulfilled promise by Vera Lynn, the father of Pinky did not get on the train of war survivors. Pinky, to overcome his disappointment, takes refuge in his mental oasis. It is located next to the train tracks at the station. It is waiting for him. He walks toward there and he sits down to watch television.

Luis Carlos Molina Acevedo

The dictator

The two men drag to Pink from hotel to the limousine in the basement. The two men sit to Pink in the back seat. The singer is in agony. His body is a blur mass of flesh eaten by worms. Old Pink died. New Pink takes the flesh eaten by worms and takes it away with his hands. He becomes the dictator. Inside the shell of rotting flesh, it was nested a skinhead. Pink is now the dictator of the hammers in X. He goes with an entourage of soldiers down the aisle toward the stage. Before entering, he raises a child in his arms. He kisses the baby. It is the essential ingredient of a dictator of seeming a sympathetic person, even if not. That attracts the sympathy of the people. He stands at the auditorium. The musician is no longer open to the public. Now his gaze is defiant. His erect body is ready for battle. In the background sounds the song "In the Flesh":

So ya, thought ya

Might like to go to the show.

To feel that warm thrill of confusion,

That space cadet glow.

I've got some bad news for you sunshine,

Pink isn't well, he stayed back at the hotel

And they sent us along as a surrogate band

We're gonna find out where you folks really stand.

Are there any queers in the theater tonight?

Get them up against the wall!

There's one in the spotlight, he doesn't look right to me,

Get him up against the wall!

That one looks Jewish!

And that one's a coon!

Who let all of this riff-raff into the room?

There's one smoking a joint,

And another with spots!

If I had my way,

I'd have all of you shot!

When the dictator is inside the rotting flesh (In the Flesh), Pink has his mission clear. He must restore the lost order at concerts. "Who let all of this riff-raff into the room?" This rabble interferes in the communication between the musicians and the fans. They only bother those who are actually interested in the concert. The mob should be shot. This way, the autistic order will be guaranteed into mental world of Pink. The mob has difficulty communicating his emotions, feelings and thoughts. In the background sounds the song "Run Like Hell":

You better make your face up in

Your favorite disguise.

With your button down lips and your

Roller blind eyes.

Is There Anybody Out The Wall?

With your empty smile and your hungry heart.

Feel the bile rising from your guilty past.

With your nerves in tatters

As the cockleshell shatters

And the hammers batter down the door.

You better run.

You better run all day and run all night.

And keep your dirty feelings deep inside.

And if you're taking your girlfriend out tonight

You better park the car well out of sight.

Cause if they catch you in the back seat

Trying to pick her locks,

They're gonna send you back to mother

In a cardboard box.

You better run.

The public has blurred faces, masks. The skinheads pursue persons with dogs in the tunnel. The windows of the shops go to be broken. People are beaten with bats. The establishment of the new order is in progress. Pink is willing to command the operation personally. In the background sounds the song "Waiting for the Worms":

One, two, three, all (Eins, zwei, drei, alle.)

Ooooh, you cannot reach me now

Ooooh, no matter how you try

Goodbye, cruel world, it's over

Walk on by.

Sitting in a bunker here behind my wall

Waiting for the worms to come.

In perfect isolation here behind my wall
Waiting for the worms to come.

Waiting to cut out the deadwood.

Waiting to clean up the city.

Waiting to follow the worms.

Waiting to put on a black shirt.

Waiting to weed out the weaklings.

Waiting to smash in their windows
And kick in their doors.

Waiting for the final solution
To strengthen the strain.

Waiting to follow the worms.

Waiting to turn on the showers
And fire the ovens.

Waiting for the queers and the coons
and the reds and the Jews.

Waiting to follow the worms.

A truck arrives with soldiers of the hammer. The skinheads are demolishing a fence. Soldiers march. "Britain is the best," the hammers say in their confrontation with the police. Nazism had to be in Britain from beginning seemed to be the complaint of the hordes of the hammers in X. Things would have been different if the premise had been true before.

A Neanderthal hits a man with a bone until to burst the skull. The head explodes in blood. This sequence of animated images is shown repeatedly in the film. Here, when the skinheads take control of the city, again, the sequence is interleaved. But this time, the soldier becomes a Neanderthal of the hammer.

Is There Anybody Out The Wall?

Again, he hits the man's head until it bursts in blood. The song "Waiting for the Worms" is sounded in the background:

Would you like to see Britannia

Rule again, my friend?

All you have to do is follow the worms.

Would you like to send our colored cousins

Home again, my friend?

All you need to do is follow the worms.

***

The worms will gather outside Brixton Bus Station.

Let's move to the 12:00 to the street Stockwll

Abad Street ... Twelve minutes before three

We are on Lambeth Road towards Vauxhall Bridge

Now, when we get to Westminster County area,

It is quite possible that we can find some

The way they go

Hammer! Hammer...!

A sequence of images of worms is inserted. The worms become a skull and this, a hammer. The hammer is multiplied. The parade of hammers is synchronized with voice "Hammer!" in military march rhythm. The order has been restored. There will be no more autistic attacks. The crisis of miscommunication is over.

Luis Carlos Molina Acevedo

IS THERE ANYBODY IN THE WALL?

The film "The Wall" offers a great paradox for the spectator. On the one hand, the protagonist Pink wonders if anyone is outside of the wall, if there is something beyond his mental world. The responses received do not fit his expectations and he continues with the question in the hope of someday receiving an appropriate response. "Your lips move but I can not hear what you say."

The great paradox is presented when to the protagonist is asked from the other side of the wall, if there is anybody on this side of the wall. It is asked to Pink if there is someone inside the wall. And interestingly, from this side is not provided answers. That's the great paradox. A deaf asks to a deaf if anybody is out there and, in turn, a deaf asks a deaf if anybody is in there. The paradox may be greater if it is considered in terms of nowhere. Nothingness, emptiness, the absence of all being, asks if anybody is out there.

Three people asked to Pink if anybody is in there:

1. The wife (32:49)

Luis Carlos Molina Acevedo

2. The dirty woman (45:22)

3. The manager (69:01)

116

Wife

A sequence where Pink is preparing to build a marijuana cigarette is shown. Then, it switches to a room with Pink at the piano. The wife enters. She comes of working. She asks:

"Hello. Hello. Is there anybody in there?"

She passes his hand by front of the eyes of Pink. The musician raises his eyes drugged. He tries to look at her, but his eyes are gone, lost. It is the look of autism. He is looking at the world as if it were in his mind. The wife speaks again, trying to make contact with him, to communicate:

"Do you remember me? I'm the one from the Registry Office."

Eyes of Pink keep lost, empty. He does not see toward out. He looks within himself. The woman gives up and walks away.

Luis Carlos Molina Acevedo

The dirty woman

Pink is in the apartment of the caravan for the tour. The dirty woman enters behind him, looking for an autograph on an album of the band. She is surprised to see how an apartment in a trailer exceeds in size her apartment for five women. She is surprised with the amount of things at that place. From out of the trailer, no one would imagine so many amenities there. It has everything one needs to live from this side of the wall. The woman did not stop talking:

"You like the tube, hub?"

"Can I get a drink of water?"

"Can I get a drink of water?"

"Oh, wow, look at this tub! Wanna take a bath?"

"What are you watching?"

"Hello? Hello?"

The dirty woman, as before his wife, also passes his hands front of the eyes of Pink, looking for some vital reaction of the singer. Again, the look is lost, empty, and ajar. He seems watching television, but actually he looks within himself. For that, at the beginning of movie, the camera zooms to the right eye of Pink and goes in through it. All there is to tell, it is in the mind of Pink. The wall is the pupil. It marks the boundary between the inside and the outside of the wall.

Manager

Pink is in a hotel room, minutes before the concert. The cleaning Employee knocks on the door. There is no answer. She tries to open with her key. The safety chain is laid in the door. Nobody replied. She informed the hotel management. The manager of tour and his entourage, open the door by force. Pink is asleep in his chair watching television. The manager does not leave his astonishment when he sees the state of things in the hotel room:

"Fuck me."

"He's gone completely around the bleedin' twist."

"You vicious bastard, you never did like me, did you?"

"And get you on your feet again", says the hotel manager.

The hotel manager makes claims to the manager of the tour. The concern, of the hotel manager, grows when paramedics placed an oxygen mask to Pink.

"The boy's an asthmatic", says the manager of the tour.

"Asthmatic!?" asks the hotel manager, seeing to Pink almost dead.

"Relax"

"I'll need some information first" says the doctor.

"He's an artist!" says the manager of the tour, trying to reassure the hotel manager. He says it as if taking hallucinogens were permitted by law for artists.

The doctor injects adrenaline to Pink in an effort to wake him from his coma by intoxication. At that time, the first sequence of images about worms is sandwiched in the film. Pink has started to die. Adrenaline did not wake him. Adrenaline dispatched him to the other side of the wall. The movement of Pink's eye is a reaction to Adrenaline. The manager of the tour says:

"He's coming around"

"That'll keep you going through the show"

"There, you see?"

"Come on, it's time to go"

"How do you feel?" the manager asks while two of his men try to open the eyes of Pink by force.

The movement of the eyelids of Pink, it was only a reflex reaction to adrenaline. The eyelids are opened by force and then, they see some eyes empty as none. These eyes no longer need be ajar to look inward. Now, they are seeing toward inside all the time. From that place, there is no answer to the question of the manager.

Bibliography

INSIDE OUT: A Personal History of Pink Floyd. Nick mason. Edited by Philip Dodd. Phoenix. 312pp.

DENTRO DE PINK FLOYD: El largo y extraño viaje hacia el éxito de un grupo mítico. Nick Mason. Ebookmundo. 2015. 1299pp.

Pink Floyd: Historia, cronología y letras. Ricardo Zotelo. Bubok. 149pp.

La Odisea de Pink Floy. La historia definitiva del grupo por muchos años. Editorial Ronbinbook, ediciones. Traducción. Eduardo Hojean. 2004, 317pp.

Guía musical de Pink Floyd. Andy Mabbett. 180pp.

Pink Floyd's THE WALL: A Complete Analysis copyrighted by Bret Urick 1997 - 1999. Traducción del inglés al español por Eddio Pinar, 2004. Formato HTML y PDF por Fernando "Rocha", 2004 y 2005 respectivamente. 27pp.

SOUND INVESTMENTS: Pink Floyd's Nick Mason. Words by Tom Hoare. Photos by Bex Wade, unless stated. 2014. 10pp.

Made in the USA
Middletown, DE
07 December 2020